Curly Cherries

Tony Mitton
Illustrated by Jo Brooker
Photographed by Keith Lillis

Rigby®
A Harcourt Achieve Imprint

www.Rigby.com
1-800-531-5015

2

3

Level AA
Animal Fantasy

Literacy by Design Leveled Readers: *Curly and the Cherries*

Photo Credits: Keith Lillis

Illustration Credits: Jo Brooker

ISBN-13: 978-1-4189-3316-6
ISBN-10:   1-4189-3316-3

Printed in China
1A 2 3 4 5 6 7 8 985 13 12 11 10 09 08 07

Fiction
Science
LEVEL
AA
Social Studies

Animal Fantasy

Literacy
by Design

Rigby®
A Harcourt Achieve Imprint

ISBN-13:978-1-4189-3316-6   **GK**
ISBN-10:   1-4189-3316-3

9 781418 933166

90000